Copyright © 2024

Published in the United States of America, 2024

Legal Notice: This book is copyright protected. This book is only for personal use. All rights reserved. No portion of this book may be reproduced, stored in a retrieval system, or transmitted in any form or by any means – electronic, mechanical, photocopy, recording, or any other – except for brief quotations in a book review, without the prior written permission of the author or publisher.

For more information, contact www.smartmindpublishing.com
First edition, 2024
ISBN 978-1-916662-27-8 (paperback)
ISBN 978-1-916662-28-5 (hardcover)

Author's Bookstore: www.SmartMindPublishing.com
Email: hello@smartmindpublishing.com

HALLOWEEN GOALS

HALLOWEEN BUCKET LIST

HALLOWEEN TRADITIONS

HALLOWEEN IDEAS

At home

GRAND SPOOKY ENTERANCE
CARVED PUMPKINS
HIDDEN SPOOKS / ANIMATRONICS
PHOTOBOOTH SET UP & PROPS
LIGHTS (DECORATIVE & GENERAL
SPEAKERS & LAPTOP
SCARY BATHROOM
HALLOWEEN TAPE, HAY STACK & WEB

Entertainment

COSTUMES (MUST FOR EVERYONE)
FUNNY QUIZ WITH PRIZES
1 DRINKING GAME
BOB THE APPLE (MUST TRADITION)
HALLOWEEN PLAYLIST
2 FUN KIDS GAMES
LATEST MUSIC PLAYLIST

YOUR IDEAS:

HALLOWEEN MUST HAVES

Safety

FIRST AID KIT & FLASHLIGHTS FULLY CHARGED MOBILE COSTUME FIX KIT EMERGENCY CONTACT LIST PETS DRESSED UP AND SAFE HANGOVER PILLS & THROW UP BAGS KEEP SAFE ANYTHING BREAKABLE CABS FOR FREE-SPIRITED GUESTS

Snacks and drinks

CANDY
STOCK OF BEVERAGES (BOTH KINDS)
DRINK DISPENSER
SNACK WITH HALLOWEENY NAMES
NAPKINS AND PAPER TOWELS
TRASH BINS WITH LIDS
EXTRA TOILET PAPER
DISPOSABLE CUPS, PLATES & SPOONS

SEPTEMBER PLANNER

MON	TUE	WED	THURS	FRI	SAT	SUN

GOALS FOR THE MONTH:

OCTOBER PLANNER

MON	TUE	WED	THURS	FRI	SAT	SUN

GOALS FOR THE MONTH:

HALLOWEEN WEEK

MON	TUE	WED	THURS	FRI	SAT	SUN

GOALS	NOTES

HALLOWEN DAILY PLANNER

TO DO

PRIORITIES

REMINDERS

NOTES

HALLOWEN DAILY PLANNER

TO DO

PRIORITIES

○ _____

○ _____

○ _____

REMINDERS

NOTES

HALLOWEN DAILY PLANNER

TO DO

PRIORITIES

REMINDERS

NOTES

HALLOWEN DAILY PLANNER

TO DO

PRIORITIES

○ _____
○ _____
○ _____

REMINDERS

NOTES

HALLOWEN DAILY PLANNER

TO DO

PRIORITIES

○ _____

○ _____

○ _____

REMINDERS

NOTES

HALLOWEN DAILY PLANNER

TO DO

PRIORITIES

○ _____

○ _____

○ _____

REMINDERS

NOTES

HALLOWEN DAILY PLANNER

TO DO

PRIORITIES

REMINDERS

NOTES

HALLOWEN DAILY SCHEDULE

TIME		TASKS
AM		
PM		

MENU OF THE DAY

PRIORITIES

NOTES

HALLOWEN DAILY SCHEDULE

TIME		TASKS
AM		
PM		

MENU OF THE DAY

PRIORITIES

NOTES

HALLOWEN DAILY SCHEDULE

TIME		TASKS
AM		
PM		

MENU OF THE DAY

PRIORITIES

NOTES

HALLOWEN DAILY SCHEDULE

TIME		TASKS
AM		
PM		

MENU OF THE DAY

PRIORITIES

NOTES

HALLOWEEN DAILY SCHEDULE

TIME		TASKS
AM		
PM		

MENU OF THE DAY

PRIORITIES

NOTES

HALLOWEN DAILY SCHEDULE

TIME		TASKS
AM		
PM		

MENU OF THE DAY

PRIORITIES

NOTES

HALLOWEN DAILY SCHEDULE

TIME		TASKS
AM		
PM		

MENU OF THE DAY

PRIORITIES

NOTES

HALLOWEEN REMINDERS

- [ ] ....
- [ ] ....
- [ ] ....
- [ ] ....
- [ ] ....
- [ ] ....
- [ ] ....
- [ ] ....
- [ ] ....
- [ ] ....
- [ ] ....
- [ ] ....
- [ ] ....
- [ ] ....
- [ ] ....
- [ ] ....
- [ ] ....
- [ ] ....

HALLOWEEN TO DO LIST

HALLOWEEN DECORATIONS

DECORATING IDEAS

SHOPPING LIST

○
○
○
○
○
○
○
○
○
○
○
○
○
○

NOTES

HALLOWEEN DECORATIONS

INSIDE

SUPPLIES NEEDED

PUMPKIN CARVERY

PUMPKIN BUDGET

TYPE/ITEM	QTY	AMOUNT
		TOTAL

NOTES

PUMPKIN CARVERY IDEAS

Draw / decorate these pumpkins with faces that need to be carved, painted, etc.

PUMPKIN CARVERY

PUMPKIN BUDGET

TYPE/ITEM	QTY	AMOUNT
	TOTAL	

NOTES

PUMPKIN CARVERY IDEAS

Draw / decorate these pumpkins with faces that need to be carved, painted, etc.

HALLOWEEN COSTUMES

FOR: _____
COSTUME NAME: _____
IDEA: _____
_____
_____

SUPPLIES: _____
_____
_____
_____

FOR: _____
COSTUME NAME: _____
IDEA: _____
_____
_____

SUPPLIES: _____
_____
_____
_____

NOTES

HALLOWEEN COSTUMES

FOR: _____
COSTUME NAME: _____
IDEA: _____
_____
_____

SUPPLIES: _____
_____
_____
_____

FOR: _____
COSTUME NAME: _____
IDEA: _____
_____
_____

SUPPLIES: _____
_____
_____
_____

NOTES

HALLOWEEN COSTUMES

FOR: _____
COSTUME NAME: _____
IDEA: _____
_____
_____

SUPPLIES: _____
_____
_____
_____

FOR: _____
COSTUME NAME: _____
IDEA: _____
_____
_____

SUPPLIES: _____
_____
_____
_____

NOTES

HALLOWEEN COSTUMES

FOR: _____
COSTUME NAME: _____
IDEA: _____
_____
_____

SUPPLIES: _____
_____
_____
_____

FOR: _____
COSTUME NAME: _____
IDEA: _____
_____
_____

SUPPLIES: _____
_____
_____
_____

NOTES

PARTY CHECKLIST

DATE + TIME
Decide on the date and time of the party

HALLOWEEN PARTY DATE: _____

SETUP DATE + TIME: _____

GUESTS ARRIVAL TIME: _____

ASSISTANCE
Determine who is on your "help list"

- ☐ **Delegate tasks**
- ☐ **Appoint someone in charge of RSVP handling**
- ☐ **Get a DIY team in place**
- ☐ **Complete all DIY projects two weeks before the party**
- ☐ **Decide on games, activities and entertainment**
- ☐ **Delegate responsibilities for the day of the party**
- ☐ **Put someone in charge of music (create a playlist)**
- ☐ **Form a decorating team to help with setup**
- ☐ **Ask a few people to help clean up after the party**

BUDGET
Create a party budget for the event

- ☐ **Set up the budget**
- ☐ **Do a thorough breakdown of the budget**
- ☐ **Determine who will manage budget and expenses**
- ☐ **Discuss budget with anyone who is contributing to the party**

VENUE
Decide where the party will be held (if anywhere else than your home)

- ☐ **Reserve venue if necessary**
- ☐ **Meet with venue to discuss food and other arrangements**
- ☐ **Check venue for parking, accessibility, space, where to place decorations**
- ☐ **If at someone else's home, make sure there is ample parking space**

PARTY CHECKLIST

THEME
Decide on the style + decor of the party

- ◯ Decide on a theme
- ◯ Choose decor to compliment the style of the party
- ◯ Go shop for necessary decor items
- ◯ Choose centerpieces and other items for tables
- ◯ Order rental items if needed (chairs, tables, tent hire, etc.)
- ◯ Order decorative items where applicable
- ◯ Having a photo booth? Organize it!

FOOD + BEVERAGES
Decide on catering options for the party

- ◯ See budget and determine overall cost/money available for catering
- ◯ Plan menu
- ◯ Make shopping list of food and drinks
- ◯ Order food (or organize it with the venue if applicable)
- ◯ Purchase/rent crockery and cutlery if needed
- ◯ Check in with people who offered to make/bring food for the party
- ◯ Having a candy table? Organize it!

INVITATIONS
Make invitations + handle RSVPs

- ◯ Compile a guest list and get all necessary contact info
- ◯ Design/order invitations
- ◯ Send out invitations - include a map of the Trick or Treat Route
- ◯ Leave space on invitations for song suggestions (optional)
- ◯ Let distant guests know via phone or email
- ◯ Keep thorough record of RSVPs and guest totals
- ◯ Ask guests about dietary requirements / food allergies on invitations
- ◯ Remind guests to dress up for the party - best costume wins a prize!
- ◯ Mention if guests have to bring something along…

PARTY CHECKLIST

TRANSPORTATION
Decide how everyone will be transported for Trick or Treat (if driving, not walking)

- ○ Ask people with trucks or big cars to help transport kids/adults
- ○ Decide on the best route to drive for Trick or Treat (give map to drivers)
- ○ Ask drivers to keep track of who is travelling with them (so no one is left behind)

ADDITIONAL THINGS TO DO...

- ○
- ○
- ○
- ○
- ○
- ○
- ○

- ○
- ○
- ○
- ○
- ○
- ○
- ○

NOTES

_____
_____
_____
_____
_____
_____

HALLOWEEN PARTY BRAINSTORMING

Details

Party Type/ Theme: _____

Date and Time: _____

Venue: _____

Menu:

Decorations:

Notes:

Favors:
☆ ☆ ☆ ☆ ☆

HALLOWEEN GUEST LIST

HALLOWEEN INVITATION

Dear, _____

You are invited to _____ Party

Where, _____

_____

When, _____

RSVP

Phone _____

Email _____

Additional Information

INVITATION WORKSHEET

ENVELOPE ADDRESSING EXAMPLE

INVITATION WORDING EXAMPLE

BOO!

HALLOWEEN GAME IDEAS

GAME & ACTIVITIES

PARTY THEME IDEAS

DECORATION IDEAS

ITEMS I HAVE:

- [ ]
- [ ]
- [ ]
- [ ]
- [ ]
- [ ]
- [ ]
- [ ]
- [ ]
- [ ]
- [ ]
- [ ]

ITEMS I NEED TO GET:

- [ ]
- [ ]
- [ ]
- [ ]
- [ ]
- [ ]
- [ ]
- [ ]
- [ ]
- [ ]
- [ ]
- [ ]

GAME & ACTIVITIES

GAME & ACTIVITY: _____

INSTRUCTIONS: _____

_____

_____

SUPPLIES NEEDED: _____

_____

_____

GAME & ACTIVITY: _____

INSTRUCTIONS: _____

_____

_____

SUPPLIES NEEDED: _____

_____

_____

NOTES

CHOSEN GAME LIST

HALLOWEEN MOVIE CHECKLIST

- [ ] MONSTER HOUSE
- [ ] THE CORPSE BRIDE
- [ ] HOTEL TRANSYLVANIA
- [ ] HOCUS POCUS
- [ ] LABYRINTH
- [ ] HARRY POTTER
- [ ] WITCHES
- [ ] THE ADDAMS FAMILY
- [ ] ET
- [ ] CASPER
- [ ] IT'S THE GREAT PUMPKIN CHARLI BROWN
- [ ] MONSTER HOUSE
- [ ] CORALINE
- [ ] BEETLEJUICE
- [ ] EDWARD SCISSORHANDS
- [ ] NIGHTMARE BEFORE CHRISTMAS
- [ ] FRANKENWEENIE

HALLOWEEN MUSIC

SONG NAME	ARTIST	DURATION

HALLOWEEN FUN ACTIVITIES

FUN THINGS TO DO

- _____
- _____
- _____
- _____

GAMES TO PLAY

- _____
- _____
- _____
- _____

DIY PROJECTS

- _____
- _____
- _____
- _____

NOTES

HALLOWEEN FUN ACTIVITIES

FUN THINGS TO DO

- _____
- _____
- _____
- _____

GAMES TO PLAY

- _____
- _____
- _____
- _____

DIY PROJECTS

- _____
- _____
- _____
- _____

NOTES

HALLOWEEN TRICK OR TREAT CHECKLIST

KIDS WITH PARENTS

- [ ] 1. COSTUME
- [ ] 2. TRICK OR TREAT BAG
- [ ] 3. FLASHLIGHT AND/OR GLOW-STICKS
- [ ] 4. COMFORTABLE SHOES
- [ ] 5. WATER
- [ ] 6. CHARGED CELLPHONE

TEENS WITH FRIENDS

ALL OF THE ABOVE AND THE FOLLOWING:

- [ ] 7. REFLECTIVE STRIP OR TAPE
- [ ] 8. EMERGENCY CONTRACT CARD
- [ ] 9. TRICK OR TREAT ROUTE GIVEN TO PARENTS
- [ ] 10. DESIGNED TIME TO BE HOME
- [ ]

NOTES

HALLOWEEN TRICK OR TREAT

DATE:	ADULTS	CHILDREN
TIME:		

ROUTE

CANDY PURCHASED	AMOUNT	PRICE

HALLOWEEN TRICK OR TREAT

DATE:	ADULTS	CHILDREN
TIME:		

ROUTE

CANDY PURCHASED	AMOUNT	PRICE

HALLOWEEN TRICK OR TREAT

DATE:

TIME:

ADULTS

CHILDREN

ROUTE

CANDY PURCHASED	AMOUNT	PRICE

HALLOWEEN MENU PLANNER

APPETIZERS

_____
_____
_____
_____
_____
_____

DRINKS

_____
_____
_____
_____
_____
_____

SALADS

_____
_____
_____
_____
_____
_____

DESSERTS

_____
_____
_____
_____
_____
_____

MAIN DISHES

_____
_____
_____
_____
_____
_____

TREATS

_____
_____
_____
_____
_____
_____

HALLOWEEN RECIPE

Details

Serves:

Prep time:

Cook time:

Oven time:

Title

Notes

Ingredients

Directions:

Tips

Tools

HALLOWEEN RECIPE

Details

Serves:

Prep time:

Cook time:

Oven time:

Title

Notes

Ingredients

Directions:

Tips

Tools

HALLOWEEN RECIPE

Details

Serves:

Prep time:

Cook time:

Oven time:

Title

Notes

Ingredients

Directions:

Tips

Tools

HALLOWEEN RECIPE

Details

Serves:

Prep time:

Cook time:

Oven time:

Title

Notes

Ingredients

Directions:

Tips

Tools

HALLOWEEN RECIPE

Details

Serves:

Prep time:

Cook time:

Oven time:

Title

Notes

Ingredients

Directions:

Tips

Tools

HALLOWEEN SHOPPING LIST

Clothing & Accessories

- ☐ _____
- ☐ _____
- ☐ _____
- ☐ _____
- ☐ _____
- ☐ _____
- ☐ _____

Clothing & Accessories

- ☐ _____
- ☐ _____
- ☐ _____
- ☐ _____
- ☐ _____
- ☐ _____
- ☐ _____

Decorations

- ☐ _____
- ☐ _____
- ☐ _____
- ☐ _____
- ☐ _____
- ☐ _____
- ☐ _____

Miscellaneous

- ☐ _____
- ☐ _____
- ☐ _____
- ☐ _____
- ☐ _____
- ☐ _____
- ☐ _____

Food & Drinks

- ☐ _____
- ☐ _____
- ☐ _____
- ☐ _____
- ☐ _____
- ☐ _____
- ☐ _____

Other

- ☐ _____
- ☐ _____
- ☐ _____
- ☐ _____
- ☐ _____
- ☐ _____
- ☐ _____

HALLOWEEN SHOPPING LIST

FOOD　　　　　　　　**WHERE TO BUY**　　　　　　　**PRICE**

☐ _____　_____　_____
☐ _____　_____　_____
☐ _____　_____　_____
☐ _____　_____　_____
☐ _____　_____　_____
☐ _____　_____　_____

DRINKS

☐ _____　_____　_____
☐ _____　_____　_____
☐ _____　_____　_____
☐ _____　_____　_____
☐ _____　_____　_____
☐ _____　_____　_____

SUPPLIES

☐ _____　_____　_____
☐ _____　_____　_____
☐ _____　_____　_____
☐ _____　_____　_____
☐ _____　_____　_____
☐ _____　_____　_____
☐ _____　_____　_____
☐ _____　_____　_____

TOTAL

MY HALLOWEEN TO DO LIST

THINGS TO MAKE

THINGS TO BAKE

THINGS TO BUY

THINGS TO DO

MY HALLOWEEN TO DO LIST

THINGS TO MAKE

THINGS TO BAKE

THINGS TO BUY

THINGS TO DO

HALLOWEEN CHECKLIST

NOTES

HALLOWEEN BUDGET

THIS YEAR HALLOWEEN BUDGET: _____

ACTUAL AMOUNT SPEND: _____

ITEM	BUDGETED	ACTUAL	DIFFERENCE

HALLOWEEN EXPENSES

DESCRIPTION	DATE	AMOUNT	PRICE

TOTAL

IMPORTANT NOTES

MONDAY

TUESDAY

WEDNESDAY

THURSDAY

FRIDAY

SATURDAY

SUNDAY

ADDITIONAL NOTES

IMPORTANT NOTES

MONDAY

TUESDAY

WEDNESDAY

THURSDAY

FRIDAY

SATURDAY

SUNDAY

ADDITIONAL NOTES

HALLOWEEN
PHOTOS

make memories that last forever!

HALLOWEEN NOTES

HALLOWEEN NOTES

HALLOWEEN NOTES

HALLOWEEN NOTES

HALLOWEEN NOTES

HALLOWEEN NOTES

HALLOWEEN NOTES

HALLOWEEN NOTES

HALLOWEEN NOTES

HALLOWEEN NOTES

HALLOWEEN NOTES

HALLOWEEN JOURNAL

HALLOWEEN JOURNAL

HALLOWEEN JOURNAL

HALLOWEEN JOURNAL

HALLOWEEN JOURNAL

HALLOWEEN JOURNAL

HALLOWEEN JOURNAL

HALLOWEEN JOURNAL

HALLOWEEN JOURNAL

HALLOWEEN JOURNAL

HALLOWEEN JOURNAL

HALLOWEEN JOURNAL

www.ingramcontent.com/pod-product-compliance
Lightning Source LLC
Chambersburg PA
CBHW081622100526
44590CB00021B/3560